Secret Agent Y.O.U.

The Official Guide to Secret Codes, Disguises, Surveillance, and More!

Spymaster **Helaine Becker**

Spy Art by **Dave Whamond**

MAPLE
TREE
PRESS

Maple Tree Press Inc.
51 Front Street East, Suite 200, Toronto, Ontario M5E 1B3
www.mapletreepress.com

Distributed in Canada by Raincoast Books
9050 Shaughnessy Street, Vancouver, British Columbia V6P 6E5

Distributed in the United States by Publishers Group West
1700 Fourth Street, Berkeley, California 94710

Dedication
For Black Lotus and Count Conundrum

Cataloguing in Publication Data
Becker, Helaine, 1961-
  Secret agent Y.O.U. : the official guide to secret codes, disguises,
  surveillance, and more! / Helaine Becker ; illustrated by Dave Whamond.

Includes index.
ISBN-10: 1-897066-68-6 (bound) / ISBN-13: 978-1-897066-68-3 (bound)
ISBN-10: 1-897066-69-4 (pbk.) / ISBN-13: 978-1-897066-69-0 (pbk.)

  1. Spies—Juvenile literature. 2. Espionage—Juvenile literature.
  3. Cryptography—Juvenile literature. I. Whamond, Dave II. Title.

UB270.5.B43 2006   j327.12   C2006-900887-6

Design & art direction: Word & Image Design Studio
Illustrations: Dave Whamond

We acknowledge the financial support of the Canada Council for the Arts, the Ontario Arts Council, the Government of Canada through the Book Publishing Industry Development Program (BPIDP), and the Government of Ontario through the Ontario Media Development Corporation's Book Initiative for our publishing activities.

ONTARIO ARTS COUNCIL
CONSEIL DES ARTS DE L'ONTARIO

Printed in Hong Kong

A   B   C   D   E   F

CONCEALED INSIDE

Do You Have What It Takes?

Not everyone is cut out to be a spy. Successful spies need a rare combination of daring and caution. They need to be physically fit, and they need to be smart, creative, and able to follow directions to the letter (coded letter, of course). Most important, they need to have the right personality for the job.

Before you would be admitted to a spy school, you would most likely be given a personality test. Based on your results, you might be assigned to one of the many aspects of espionage work, such as analyzing Internet message traffic, code breaking, or forensics. Would you make the grade? Take the classified quiz on the next page to find out if you can become a **Young Operative Undercover**

Spy School Entrance Exam

Use a separate piece of paper to record your answers.
Good luck, hopefuls!

1. Did you gather pencil and paper to record your answers, or were you planning to write them in the book?
   a. Yes, I am scoring my answers on a separate piece of paper.
   b. No, I was planning to write my answers in the book.
   NOTE: If you answered **a**, continue with the exam. If you answered **b**, you automatically FAIL the exam. A spy **must** follow instructions at all times.

2. When a friend tells me a secret:
   a. I blab it immediately to everyone I know.
   b. I keep it for a while, then maybe I'll tell one other friend.
   c. Secret, what secret? No one told me a secret!

3. I consider myself to be…
   a. …absolutely terrific looking.
   b. …average in appearance.
   c. …scary.

4. How well do you get along with other people?
   a. I'm the life of the party.
   b. I'd rather be alone than with other people.
   c. Fine—I'm neither the most popular nor least popular kid in my class.

5. How smart are you?
   a. I'm tops in my class.
   b. I'm smart, but I'm not the smartest kid in the school.
   c. I don't understand the question.

6. Are you…
   a. …a leader?
   b. …a follower?
   c. …independent—you tend to go your own way?

7. How would you describe your emotions?
   a. I'm a pretty emotional and intense person.
   b. I'm content most of the time.
   c. I think emotions are for wimps.

8. How would you describe your energy level?
   a. High—I can go nonstop from dawn to midnight.
   b. Average.
   c. I am somewhat sluggish—I tire easily.

9. In addition to English, how many other languages can you speak well?

Your Secret Spy Score

1. a:1 b:0
2. a:0 b:1 c:5
3. a:2 b:5 c:1
4. a:3 b:1 c:5
5. a:5 b:3 c:0
6. a:3 b:5 c:1
7. a:2 b:5 c:1
8. a:5 b:2 c:0
9. 5 points for each additional language

Want to decode your score results? New spies must go to the next page.

Your Spy-Q

Locate which range your exam score (from previous page) fits into, and find out what your future might be in the spy world.

7-14 — Public Relations Director, or Technical Analyst.

With your flair and smarts, the best secret agent jobs for you would be either in communications—dealing with the media and promoting the service to new recruits, or behind the scenes—handling technical services such as computer work, electronic surveillance, or forensic analysis.

15-25 — Case Officer.

You combine the right degree of braininess with wide-ranging interests and maturity. You like adventure, but can stick to a routine. Your likability means you can succeed in a field where being able to gain access to others and win their trust is everything. Your best job might be as a case officer, running field agents who report to you.

26-45 — Spymaster.

You are an independent thinker with a logical mind and the ability to rein in your emotions. You are not afraid of new or unusual situations, but relish the challenge. While you get along well with others, you have no problem going it alone. You can do it all, so you just might be fast-tracked into a career as a spymaster, planning and overseeing worldwide missions.

46+ — Better than Bond.

Move over 007, Agent Y.O.U. is in town. With your particular blend of talents, you can be a successful field operative at home or abroad. You can see the big picture, but can handle the details too. Your ability to wait patiently is an asset, but so is your charm. Keep honing your language skills, engage in lots of activities, and read everything!

Talk the TALK

Now that you've proven that you're spy material, you'll need to familiarize yourself with spy lingo. On a separate piece of paper, match each of the examples of spookspeak with its correct definition. Check your answers on page 62.

1. Birdwatcher
2. Babysitter
3. Cobbler
4. Disinformation
5. Rolled up
6. Musician
7. Shoe
8. Sleeper
9. The take
10. Uncle
11. Mole

a) when an operation fails and an agent is arrested
b) agent living as an ordinary citizen, only activated when needed
c) false information put out by an intelligence agency to fool the enemy
d) a false passport or other identification
e) British term for a spy
f) clandestine radio operator, uses a "music box"
g) headquarters of any espionage service
h) spy who creates false passports and other documents
i) information gathered through espionage
j) bodyguard
k) agent who has infiltrated the enemy's headquarters

Spy World

Welcome to I.C.U. H.Q. Everyone in a spy network works as a team, from the top-dog spymaster to the sleeper agent. Can you match each of the agents in this scene to his or her job description? Watch out for moles from N.M.E. H.Q.!

a) Analyzes and decodes messages.

b) Collects valuable information by analyzing threads, hairs, blood samples, and other physical evidence.

c) Responsible for overseeing and running one or several operations in the field; recruits other agents.

d) Oversees staff that retrieves and examines information.

e) An enemy agent within headquarters that has access to top-secret information.

f) Invents gadgets such as infrared cameras, miniature bugs, and satellite surveillance technology.

g) Specializes in disinformation—sending out false information to confuse the enemy—and catching enemy spies.

h) Runs several spy networks and operations at once; advises and confers with top government officials.

i) Performs no activity until called upon.

j) Oversees staff that handles technology and electronics.

k) Responsible for tracking targets; favorite tools include long distance cameras, binoculars, and cars.

l) A break-in expert. Talents include lock picking, safe cracking, disguise, disabling guards and guard dogs. Collects information, such as forensic evidence, photographs, and documents.

m) Translates documents.

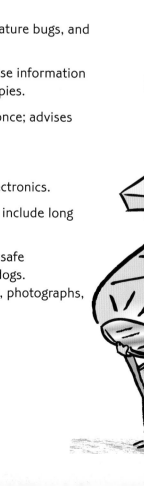

TECHNICAL OFFICER

ELECTRONICS TECHNICIANS

MOE'S BARBER

FLOWERS

Bonus: Can You Find the Jib?

An inflatable agent (yes, you read that correctly), or a blow-up dummy, replaces a real agent, allowing couriers, break-in specialists, and other field operators to escape unseen.

Fact File

Appearances Can Fool You

Want to be tops at top-secret? Cultivate appearing dull and ordinary. MI5, the British Security Service, actively looks for people who are able to blend into the background. Their application forms actually specify, "We are looking for average height, build and appearance."

I'LL HAVE A BURGER PLAIN.

The Spy's Code of Ethics

Yes, spying involves deception, betrayal, and skullduggery. But this doesn't mean that spies can be rats. In 1982, a code of ethics was developed for U.S. foreign intelligence agents. It said that agents should:
* carry out their duties in accordance with the country's laws
* carry out their duties without seeking or obtaining any personal gain
* not engage in any unauthorized activity

Don't Underestimate Her

Throughout history, women have made great spies. They were often able to sneak past officials who did not think a woman could pose a risk. During the American Civil War, Elizabeth Van Lew carried information across enemy lines hidden in a food basket, and was later honored by General Ulysses S. Grant. Betty Duvall hid secret messages in her hairdo. Mary Elisabeth Bowser, posing as an illiterate servant, served dinner to the President of the Confederacy, Jefferson Davis, and was totally ignored as she listened in on top-secret military plans.

Camp X-treme

Think summer camp is all fun and games? You wouldn't if your parents signed you up for Camp X. Located on Lake Ontario, in Canada, this ultra-secret sleepaway was really a training facility for American, British, and Canadian agents and resistance fighters in World War II.

Forget about basket making and canoing—instead, Camp X gave instruction in sabotage, counterfeiting, and code breaking. Native Iroquois hunters taught silent stalking techniques; the one-time head of the Shanghai Chinese police taught courses in martial arts; and career criminals taught lock picking.

TRAINING MISSION: Y.O.U.

It takes more than brains to be a super-snoop.
Spies need to have endurance, strength, agility, coordination, and flexibility. Do Y.O.U. have the physical skills it takes to be a super-snoop?

Brace yourself. The four rigorous training missions in this file folder have been meticulously crafted to evaluate your skills. They will require your utmost in terms of concentration, stamina, and willpower. (Pssst—they're a lot of fun too!)

Mission 2-I:
The Paris Train Challenge

You are in a train station in Paris, France, about to swap top-secret information with your courier. Out of the corner of your eye, you spot an enemy agent who is about to snap your photograph. Your cover must not be blown; you need to evade your pursuer, and fast! Your response? Duh—you run!

It simply won't do to huff and puff to the end of Track 86, then collapse in a sweaty heap. Agent Y.O.U., what is your aerobic status? Will you save the world, or get caught in the flash?

You'll Need
jump rope (optional)
stopwatch or clock with a second hand

The Challenge
▷ Jump rope or jog in place for 3 minutes without stopping.

Check your results against your Mission Report Card on page 62.

As a Secret Agent you've got to be fit
Aerobic fitness is a measure of how well your heart and lungs are able to bring oxygen to your muscles. A stronger heart means you can deliver more oxygen over a longer period of time without tiring. You will be able to run longer, swim farther, and hike deeper into enemy territory.

SKIPPITY SKIP

Mission 2-2:
Poison Dart Challenge

You are browsing in a market in Istanbul, Turkey, tailing an enemy agent. Suddenly, a poison dart disguised as a chicken drumstick comes hurtling toward you. How good is your reaction time? Will you dodge the pointy poultry or get nicked by the chick? Take this test to discover your fate.

You'll Need
tracing paper
pencil
scissors
piece of cardboard (about the size of this page)
fine-tipped marker or pen
a friend

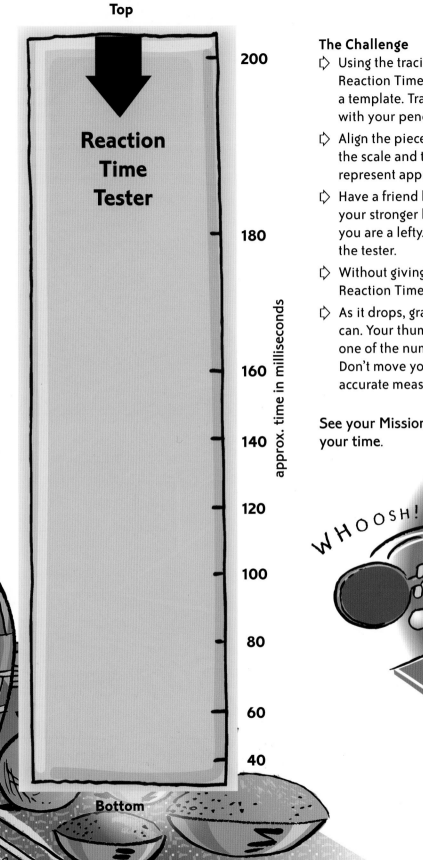

Reaction
Time
Tester

200

180

approx. time in milliseconds

160

140

120

100

80

60

40

Bottom

The Challenge

▷ Using the tracing paper and pencil, copy the official Reaction Time Tester shown at left. Cut out—you now have a template. Trace the template's shape onto the cardboard with your pencil. Cut out.

▷ Align the piece of cardboard with the tester at left to copy the scale and the arrow onto your own tester. The numbers represent approximate time, in milliseconds.

▷ Have a friend hold the reaction tester at the arrow, above your stronger hand. (Your right if you are a righty, your left if you are a lefty.) Line up your fingers with the bottom edge of the tester.

▷ Without giving you any warning, your friend will drop the Reaction Time Tester.

▷ As it drops, grab it between two fingers as quickly as you can. Your thumb and index finger should grip on or near one of the numbers of the scale marked on the tester. Tip: Don't move your hand to "chase" the timer as it falls. For an accurate measure, just close your fingers as fast as you can.

See your Mission Report Card on page 63 to evaluate your time.

WHOOSH!

Catlike or Slothful?

Do you have the lightning-fast reflexes of a professional table tennis player, or do you function in slow motion? Reaction time is largely a matter of genetics. In general, men are slightly faster than women and younger people are faster than older ones. Fatigue, hunger, poor physical fitness levels, and distraction can slow your reaction times.

Mission 2-3:
Losing the Tail

You're in the crowded stands at a championship soccer match in Manchester, England, when you notice you are being followed. You have the microdisc hidden in your retainer and must not let it fall into enemy hands.

To lose your pursuers, you must double back and forth, changing direction and leaping over obstacles as they arise. You must also avoid bumping into the spectators. Are you agile enough to shake your tail while breezing through the fans?

You'll Need
measuring tape
chalk
stopwatch or clock with a second hand
a friend
pencil and paper

The Challenge

▷ Using the chalk, draw an octagon (eight-sided "stop sign" shape) on the sidewalk. Each of the eight sides should measure 60.5 cm (24 in.).

▷ Start by standing, both feet together, in the middle of the octagon. You should be facing out, toes pointing to one of the eight sides.

▷ Your friend will yell "Go!" the moment he starts the timer. At this command, jump over the line, out of the octagon. Then immediately jump back into the middle of the octagon.

▷ Quickly turn to face the line to your immediate left and repeat the jumps. Make sure your body and toes are facing the line you are crossing at each jump.

▷ Continue, jumping out of the octagon and back in, until you have jumped across all eight sides.

▷ Repeat the entire jumping sequence, without stopping, two more times, so that you have gone around the octagon three times in total.

▷ Record the time it took to do the entire sequence of jumps on your paper.

▷ Take a break until you get your breath back. When you are ready to jump again, repeat the entire test, but this time, jump then turn to your right. Record your time for this second test on your paper.

Excellent work, Agent Y.O.U.! Add the two test scores together and check your results against your Mission Report Card on page 63.

Practice Makes Perfect

Don't worry if you're an ace when it comes to shooting hoops, but are lousy in a hockey shootout. No one is equally coordinated at every activity. Training for a specific activity will improve your performance—at that activity. To see the value of good, old-fashioned hard work, practice this octagon jump for a week or two. Retest yourself at the end of your training period and compare your scores. Did your results improve?

Mission 2-4:
The Jittery Jewel Thief Affair

You have located the radioactive diamond with which Dr. Repento has threatened to blow up the world. The diamond is protected by high security. To save the world from sure doom, you must lift the diamond off of the stand without letting it touch the radon wires that come within a hair's breadth of the stone. If you touch the wires, Ka-Pow! Can you do it? Do you have nerves of steel, or sh-sh-shaky fingers?

You'll Need
30 cm (12 in.) wide roll of aluminum foil
scissors
tape
2 popsicle sticks
wire coat hanger
pliers
sandpaper
2 "D" batteries
30 cm x 30 cm (12 in. x 12 in.) piece of cardboard
3-volt buzzer with wires attached (available in science supply shops, hardware stores or joke shops)

Mission Preparation
1 Pull out foil from the roll and measure and cut a 5 cm (2 in.) strip, the full width of the roll. Fold it in half to make a 2.5 cm x 30 cm (1 in. x 12 in.) flat strip. Repeat three times to make four matching strips.

2 Attach the popsicle sticks by overlapping the ends so they can be taped together to make a 24 cm (9½ in.) long handle. Lay the handle on one of the foil strips. Allowing 2.5 cm (1 in.) of foil to hang over

one end, wrap the handle with the foil to cover. Bend the excess foil to make a loop (about the size of a dime) and secure with tape. Set aside.

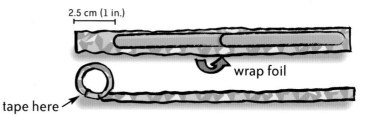

2.5 cm (1 in.)

wrap foil

tape here

3 Using one of the three remaining foil strips, connect the negative pole (the end with the minus sign) of one battery to the positive pole (with the plus sign) of the other battery. Lay each end of the foil strip across the ends of the batteries and tape the foil into place, making sure that it is snug against the batteries.

4 Stand the batteries side by side on the cardboard with the foil ends down (situate them close to the edge of the cardboard nearest you). They should stand with the positive end pointing up on the left and the negative end pointing up on the right.

5 Tape the third strip of foil to the positive end of the battery on the left. Tape the remaining strip of foil to the negative end of the battery on the right. The collection of strips and batteries should look like this:

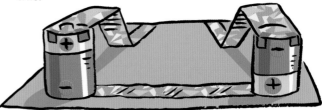

6 Carefully untwist the neck of the coat hanger using the pliers, and then straighten the whole thing out. Ask an adult for help with this step. If the hanger has a coating on it, use the sandpaper to expose the bare metal, which will allow electricity to flow freely. Be patient; patience is a spy's most important virtue. Next, bend the coat hanger to form an upside-down U with a 2.5 cm (1 in.) long flat foot on each end. Add small bends and bumps to the wire.

7 Tape one "foot" of the hanger close to the top edge of the cardboard above the battery on the left.

8 Wrap the foil running from the battery on the left around the hanger, just above the left "foot"; tape to secure. Make sure that the two metals (foil and hanger) touch snuggly.

9 Tape the black wire of the buzzer to the foil connected to the battery on the right. Direct contact between wire and foil is crucial for a successful mission.

10 Tape the red wire of the buzzer to the end of the handle on the aluminum foil loop. Make sure the wire is directly touching the foil.

11 Slip the aluminum foil loop over the unattached foot of the coat hanger. Touch the loop to the hanger. Does the buzzer buzz? If so, then everything is working properly. If the buzzer doesn't buzz, check that foil and batteries, foil and hanger, and foil and wires are metal to metal.

12 Keeping the loop around the hanger, tape the loose "foot" of the hanger to the cardboard so it stands like a dome. You have now completed your Jitters Tester.

2.5 cm (1 in.)   2.5 cm (1 in.)

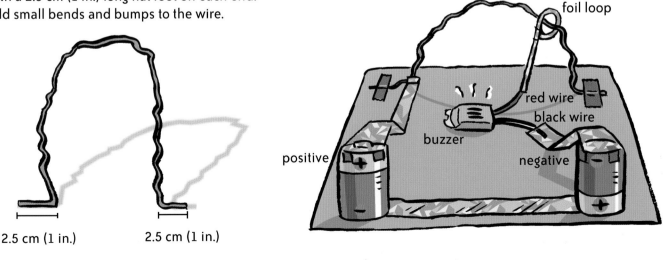

foil loop

red wire
black wire
buzzer
positive
negative

Your mission is to move the loop along the hanger's curved path, from one end to the other, without making the buzzer ring. Check your results on your Mission Report Card on page 63.

19

Fact File

Endure to Survive

During a World War II mission against the Nazis, Norwegian resistance fighter Jan Baalsrud was pushed to superhuman feats of endurance when the enemy ambushed his team. In the frigid Norwegian wilderness, and missing one shoe, Baalsrud survived an avalanche, snow blindness, the loss of a toe, and being buried alive in snow for over a week before making it across the border to safety on a reindeer-drawn sled.

DANKE
SCHÖN

The Dexterous Decorator

René Duchez was an interior decorator in Normandy, France, during World War II. He was also a member of the French Resistance, which fought against the Nazis. Duchez landed a job decorating Nazi party offices, and stole a map that revealed German military positions. He arranged to pass it on to his colleagues at a café, but when he got there a German officer was at the next table. And a few moments later, in came the German police! Luckily, the police left without any trouble. Duchez's friends were amazed at how calm he seemed, but Duchez just shrugged. When the police arrived he had simply slipped the map into the German officer's coat pocket. When the coast was clear, he helped the officer on with his coat, and helped himself to the map!

But Could He Boil an Egg?

British Royal Navy Lieutenant Commander Patrick Dalzel-Job made the fictional James Bond look like an amateur. Dalzel-Job could ski backwards, navigate a miniature submarine, and survive the riskiest parachute jumps.

Always an independent thinker, Dalzel-Job defied orders when, during a World War II Nazi bombing raid, he commandeered fishing boats and evacuated 5,000 Norwegians. He only narrowly avoided a British court martial, thanks to the grateful king of Norway, who awarded him a medal of honor.

Ninja Notes

They are the stuff of legend: Black-clad, stealthy assassins trained in Japanese martial arts. These are the ninja (the name means "stealers in"). In their remote mountain hideaways, the ninja acquired uncanny skills of stealth and strength. Training for a ninja would begin almost as soon as he could walk. Childhood games encouraged proficiency in unarmed combat, camouflage, escape, and evasion.

The Art of Disguise

Mission Invisible: A successful spy can conceal her identity while seamlessly blending into the scene. But let's be frank here. You're a kid. You can't fool anyone by dressing up as a letter carrier or a butcher. Your best disguise is as a kid that is definitely not you. You can probably identify "jocks," "skateboarders," "artsy" types, and "serious scholars" among your classmates. Choose a style that is quite different from your own. Copy the clothes, the hair, the gestures, and the speech mannerisms that kids in that group prefer. Then ask yourself, "Is that really ME in the mirror?" Nope. It's Secret Agent Y.O.U.

Stereotypical clothing and behavior act as shorthand that helps people instantly "read" you as a jock or a skateboarder, a punk, or a scholar. Complete your disguise with some of the tips below.

▷ Friends and family can recognize you even at a distance of up to 50 metres (55 yds.) by the way you walk. To change your gait, place a pebble or small marble in your shoe. This will force you to limp a bit.

▷ Change your body shape by adding padding. Strap small pillows to your belly or rolled up socks or a t-shirt to your upper arms to make you look bigger than normal. Use string or duct tape to hold them in place.

▷ Mom was right: Look taller than normal by standing up extra tall and straight. Look shorter than normal by slouching and hunching your shoulders.

▷ Sunglasses really do help disguise your identity. Grab a few different pairs and try them out for effect.

▷ Fill your pockets with authentic "pocket litter." This is the term spies use to describe the stuff we keep in our pockets every day. Pocket litter says a lot about us. If you are dressing as an artsy type, for example, you might consider a guitar pick, an artist's gray pencil eraser, and a crumpled drawing.

Creating Your Legend

Every disguise needs a "legend"—an alternate personal history that convinces others that the spy is who he says he is. To create the legend for your disguise, use these tested techniques.

1. Choose a history that you can remember. If you make your imaginary past too complicated, you'll never be able to keep your facts straight.

2. Choose a character that you can believably impersonate. Don't say you come from France unless you can really speak French and can speak English with a French accent.

3. Give yourself a hobby (preferably one you really do like!), a favorite sport (ditto), and a favorite subject at school.

Example: Your legend is that you are Mackenzie Downey, a fab soccer goalie, and you come from (fill in other city/country here). Your mom is in the military, and you have recently moved to town since she was transferred.

Before you practice your legend, do your homework (yes—even spies have homework!). Find out everything you can about the city or country you say you're from. (You can do this easily on the Web, or go to a library.) Do some research into what life is like for a kid living on a military base, so you'll be prepared for any questions. When your legend comes to life in your mind, you are ready to test it.

Test Your Legend: Sit down to dinner with your family as Mackenzie Downey. Interact with everyone as only Mackenzie would—don't even crack your cover when your little brother does that thing with his eyes that you can't stand. Together with your disguise, see if your legend can fool those who know you best.

The Code Name

When you become a spy, you give up your real name for a cover name, like Mackenzie Downey. You may also have a code name that is designed to keep both your real identity, and your cover identity, secret. Find your own code name using the spy's Official Crypto-Name Assigning Device.

If your first name begins with...	Part A of your code name is...	If your birthday falls on this day of the month...	Part B of your code name is...
A	Count, or Count de	1	Ransome
B	Twinkle	2	Gudunov
C	Dr.	3	44
D	Fred	4	Framboise
E	Tulip	5	Dolphin, or the Dolphin
F	Belle	6	Krupp
G	Shakira	7	Lotus
H	Hans	8	Percy Bythe
I	Oleg	9	Von Papen
J	Tatiana	10	Boris
K	Ignatz	11	Rembrandt
L	Hermann	12	Fandango
M	Black, or the Black	13	Tagliatelle
N	Jade	14	Conundrum
O	Miss Stella	15	Eagle Dancer
P	Madame, or Madame de	16	Landauer
Q	(No first name) or "Q"	17	Will-o'-the-Wisp
R	Mr.	18	Paradox
S	Paris	19	Blade
T	Merriwether	20	Cobra
U	Lily	21	Hanover
V	Smitty	22	Earle
W	Steele	23	Espana
X	Houston	24	Kang Sheng
Y	Walter J.	25	Hunnicut
Z	Zeno	26	Saxon
		27	Wolfgang
		28	Frederick
		29	Enigma
		30	Ionesco
		31	Medici, or de Medici

GIGGA JIGGA

The Spook's Makeup Bag

While a simple change of clothing and hairstyle may be all you need for a good disguise, a little makeup can turn it into a great one. A few basic supplies should be in every spy's bag of tricks. Collect yours, then use them to whip up these spy-cial effects.

Fake Blood

Fake blood is just about the easiest special effect makeup to do.

You'll Need
measuring cup
60 mL (¼ cup) corn syrup
small, rinsed out yogurt container
food coloring
toothpicks (or popsicle stick)

1 Pour approximately 60 mL (¼ cup) of corn syrup into a yogurt container.
2 Add food coloring. For realistic "human" blood, try 8 drops of red and 2 drops of blue. Green makes really gruesome alien blood.
3 Mix with a toothpick until the color is blended evenly. Add more food coloring if desired.
4 Apply to exposed skin with a toothpick. Example: Just below your kneecap for a skinned knee. Allow your blood to set for about 5 to 10 minutes. It will still be gooey, so make sure you're not wearing your best spy suit.

Bruises

Spying is a tough job, and you've got the bruises to show for it. Fake ones, of course.

You'll Need
deep blue powder eye shadow
charcoal or smoke gray powder eye shadow
shimmery green powder eye shadow
makeup brush

1 Use the deep blue powder eye shadow for the first layer. Apply the color to the desired area using a damp makeup brush.
2 Using your fingertips and the gray shadow, add a layer of grayish black over the blue "bruise."
3 For a realistic starting-to-fade look, touch up the edges with yellowy green eye shadow. Smudge the bruise to complete.

The very best spies leave no trace.

Prepare these recipes in a mess-friendly area, like the bathroom or outside. Wash off with soap and water, and dry with paper towels (do not use your parents' "for show" towels!).

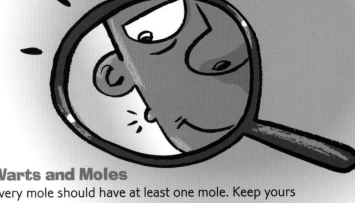

Warts and Moles

Every mole should have at least one mole. Keep yours small and subtle so you don't attract too much attention.

You'll Need
white glue
plastic spoon
small, rinsed out yogurt container
1 slice of white bread
food coloring (if desired)
flesh colored liquid makeup (optional)

1 Pour about 2 spoonfuls of glue into the yogurt container.
2 Add some food coloring to the glue. (One drop at a time, stirring with the plastic spoon, until the desired color is reached.) For a realistic flesh color, combine red and yellow. Add a little green for a brown mole. Use green or yellow for infectious-looking growths. For a nasty red wart, stick with red only.
3 Pinch a pea-sized lump from the slice of bread.
4 Plunk the bread into the glue and mix it around. Then, using your fingers, squeeze the gluey bread into a lump. The back of the lump—the part that will stick to your face, should be somewhat flattened for sticking power.
5 Place the gluey wart on your face in the desired location. Press the wart and hold it for a moment for the glue to stick. You may have to spread the glue around the edges to smooth it and make it look like it's part of your skin.
6 Allow the wart to dry for about 5 minutes. Repeat, as desired, to make additional warts and moles.
7 You can spread liquid face makeup over the "wart" and your skin to make it look more natural. Use a gentle touch to make sure you do not dislodge your growth.

Fact File

If Only He Had Cool Shades...

During World War I, Lawrence of Arabia was one of Britain's most successful spies. He dressed as a desert dweller and spoke fluent Arabic. His disguise was so good, he was even able to fool top government officials into thinking that he was the real deal. Until they noticed his eyes, that is. They were a brilliant shade of blue, a color not common among the locals. He was captured, thrown into jail, and tortured. Luckily, he escaped with his life, and his baby blues, intact!

Rock and Mole?

In 2006, British foreign intelligence agents were caught red-handed in Moscow trying to send and retrieve top-secret messages—using a rock! The rock was actually a clever disguise for a wireless communications device that allowed the spies to download classified information. The Russian police said the device, which had been planted on a busy city street, was a "wonder" that must have cost tens of millions of dollars to build.

Call Him a She-ro...

During the late 18th century, King Louis XV employed one of Frances's greatest spies— Chevalier d'Éon. His mission: Prevent Tsarina Elizabeth of Russia from signing a treaty with the king of England. D'Éon disguised himself as a charming lady, Lia de Beaumont, and was given the honored position of Court Reader for the Tsarina. Lia read from a book that contained a coded message from Louis XV. The Tsarina refused to sign the treaty with the English king, and Lia/d'Éon instantly became a hero back in France.

Silence Is Golden

When you are undercover, lock those lips! The more you say, the more likely you are to give yourself away. When the conversation is focused on you, keep your answers short and to the point. Then turn the conversation away from yourself by asking questions of the others around you. Encourage newcomers to join your circle, and put the focus on them.

A PEEK AT SURVEILLANCE

What's your next move? You're in disguise. You've got your cover story in place. It's time to begin collecting information. The first step is to learn how to OBSERVE and RECOGNIZE important details. The second is to REMEMBER them. The training missions in this chapter are real eye-openers. Do your best, Agent Y.O.U., H.Q. is watching you!

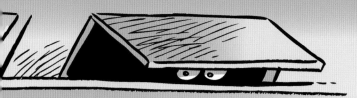

Mission 4-I:
Assess and Predict

Having outrun the rogue photographer and donned a new disguise, you are now safely on the train. Just as you thought the coast was clear, security guards enter your car. If the microdisc you are carrying is found, your cause will be lost. Do you jump, or do you sit tight?*

Secret agents like Y.O.U. need to be able to accurately assess each and every situation in which they find themselves. They are then more likely to correctly predict what might happen next. Repeat the mission below as often as you can. Record the results of your mission attempts in a journal. Do your assessment, observation, and prediction skills improve over time?

Mission Details

⇨ Go about your daily activities. Pay attention to what is going on around you.

⇨ Constantly ask yourself, what will happen next? For example, if you are waiting to cross the street at a traffic light, try and guess who, of the others waiting, will cross first.

⇨ The greater number of guesses you make, the more information you will collect on the way people behave in different situations. Gradually, you will discover you notice more of what is going on around you.

⇨ You can begin by studying this train scene closely. You will be asked questions about it later.

*In this case, your expert assessment of the surroundings and your fellow train passengers has led you to believe the guards are looking for a watch smuggler. He's the one with the nervous "tic" across the aisle from you. You decide to sit tight, the guards hustle off the smuggler, and the microdisc remains safely lodged in your cute pigtail wig.

31

Mission 4-2:
The Pattern Game

You have received orders to observe suspected double agent RV. You have been watching the goings-on through a window of an empty building across the street from RV's apartment. You must report to your superiors if you see anything out of the ordinary. At right is your journal entry after three days of observation. Do you make a report to your superiors? Or do you sit tight?

Check your answer on page 63.

Active Attention

Most of us are creatures of routine. We get up in the morning at the same time, leave for work or school at the same time, and follow the same route there and home again. By watching and observing the patterns of activity in your neighborhood, you can learn to recognize what is normal. As a result, you will be instantly aware of even a minor change in the pattern. The change may indicate something interesting is happening—something worth paying attention to!

Monday
8:30 - Walked dog
9:00 - Returned home with dog and loaf of bread
12:00 - Left for lunch at café on ground floor
1:00–3:00 - Returned to apartment, phone calls on secure line
4:00–6:00 - Took nap
6:30 - Dinner in café
7:30 - Walked dog
9:00 - Lights out

Tuesday
8:30 - Walked dog
9:00 - Returned home with dog and loaf of bread
12:00 - Left for lunch at café on ground floor
1:00–3:00 - Returned to apartment, phone calls on secure line
4:00–6:00 - Took nap
6:30 - Dinner in café
7:30 - Walked dog
9:00 - Lights out

Wednesday
8:30 - Walked dog
12:00 - Returned home with dog
3:00 - Lunch in downstairs café
4:00 - Went out without dog
4:15 - Returned home with a loaf of bread and a bottle of champagne
6:30 - Dined in café downstairs with 2 men and 1 woman wearing black suits and sunglasses
8:00 - Returned to apartment alone, drank champagne, and danced around the room
9:00 - Let dog out in rear garden
9:15 - Lights out

Mission 4-3:
Liar, Liar Pants on Fire

In this mission, you will use your observation skills to determine if someone is telling the truth or lying outright. Two suspected moles, Johnnie and Joanie, have been hauled into H.Q. for questioning.

▷ Honest people usually speak with their whole bodies. Their eyes will widen, their arms and hand gestures will emphasize their words. They may lean toward you as they speak, and they will look you in the eye.

▷ Liars talk with their mouths only. Their eyes may move quickly down and to the right. Eye contact will be fleeting, or to compensate for this tendency, they may stare.

▷ Liars also keep their body motions tight. Their arms may remain close to their bodies, and they will tend not to use as expressive gestures as their more honest pals.

▷ People who are telling the truth usually sit in a relaxed posture with the soles of both feet on the floor. Liars have a tense body, and only their heels, toes, or sides of the feet may be touching the ground.

▷ Liars have trouble knowing what to do with their hands. Watch for hands that remain hidden, in pockets, or balled up one in the other. Also watch for unusual or repeated gestures where the person frequently touches his or her mouth, nose, or eyes.

Can you tell who is lying? Check your answer on page 63.

Mission 4-4:
Mind Your Memories

Secret agents need mega-memories. You can't keep a map on your person in case you get caught—you have got to have it permanently stamped on your brain. You also need to be able to rattle off your legend, or cover story, flawlessly, anytime, anywhere. Are you a shoe-in for success, or will your memory need rebooting? Check your results on page 63.

You'll Need
this book
pencil and paper

Mission Details
Without flipping back, recall the train scene you studied three pages ago. Answer the following questions on your paper:

a) True or false: There is a microphone hidden in a potted plant.

b) How many pairs of eyes are peering out from the overhead luggage bin?

c) How many people in the train car have moustaches?

d) True or false: The lady with the poodle is wearing earrings.

e) Who has the briefcase?

f) True or false: There are more women than men on the train.

g) Is the train passing through mountains or through a village?

Use Your Senses

The more parts of your body you use when learning some new information, the easier it will be to recall that information. Imagine you need to remember how to spell the code keyword "Discombobulate." (Discombobulate: to confuse.)

■ Look at the word. **Picture it** in your mind written on a blackboard. This uses your **eyes** and your **imagination**.

■ Write the word. **Write it** in large block letters, in tiny bubble letters, in cursive. When you write, you will use your **eyes**, your sense of **touch**, and the **muscles** in your hand.

■ Spell the word **out loud**. This uses your **tongue and lips** (to say it) and your **ears** (to hear it).

■ As you recite the word, **drum out a beat** on the table. This uses your **muscles**, and your **ears**. By giving it a rhythm, you also use your **musical sense**.

■ **Act out** the word as you spell it, or do **body spelling**—as you spell the word, shape your body into each letter. This gets your **whole body** in on the act!

Spec-tacular Vision

No one likes to have an enemy agent sneak up behind them! When you wear these shades, not only will you look spy-cool, but you will also be able to see what's happening both in front of you and behind you! The secret is the mirror tucked inside the lens.

You'll Need
1 pair of inexpensive, large-framed sunglasses
ruler
flexible plastic mirrors that you can cut with scissors
   (sheets available at arts and crafts or science
    supply stores)
marker
scissors
tape
glue

1 With your ruler, measure a lens of the glasses from top to bottom, just inside the frames. This is how tall you'll need to make your mirror.

2 Measure about 2 cm ($\frac{3}{4}$ in.) for the width of the mirror. It can't cover the entire lens, because you'll still need to see forward through the glasses.

3 Using your marker, lightly draw these measurements on the back of the mirror in the shape of a rectangle.

4 Carefully cut the mirror. Test the size by fitting the mirror to the inside of the lens against the outer edge. You may need to trim the mirror to fit to the contours of the glasses.

5 Use small pieces of tape to fix the mirror into place behind the lens, with the reflective surface pointing toward your face. Test them out. The mirror should provide a small reflection of what is behind you.

6 Once you have the mirror in the right position, remove the tape and glue it to the inside of the lens, keeping the reflective surface pointing toward your face. Allow the glue to dry for about 10 minutes before embarking on your next mission.

Mission 4-5:
Operation Stealth

You are now ready to exercise your surveillance training. Remember, Agent Y.O.U., collecting information without being detected is the foremost goal of a field agent.

You'll Need
stopwatch or watch with a second hand
cunning
pen & paper

Objective
Secret Listening Device (disguised as a harmless can opener)

Enemy Operatives
Miss Stella 44 (a.k.a. Mom), Oleg de Medici (a.k.a. Dad), Twinkle Fandango and Dr. Ransome (a.k.a. siblings)

Target Location
Top left kitchen drawer.

Mission Details

This mission must be completed during a time of high activity around the Target Location (e.g. dinner hour). The stealthiest spy will succeed without arousing the suspicions of the Enemy Operatives.

▷ Start stopwatch in bedroom.

▷ Make your way to the Target Location.

▷ Remove Objective from location. Return to bedroom.

▷ Disable the Secret Listening Device by turning handle three times to the right, six times to the left, four times to the right.

▷ Return to Target Location.

▷ Return Objective to hiding place.

▷ Return to bedroom. Stop stopwatch.

▷ Record your time.

See if you can improve your time by repeating the exercise two or three times in a week.

Fact File

I Spy with My Union Eye...

Henry Harrison Young began his career as a spy for the Union army during the American Civil War. Despite his small size and boyish appearance, he quickly gained a reputation for daring and cunning. His favorite tactic was to capture enemy generals. One Confederate officer, General Jubal Early, so feared kidnapping by Young that he doubled the number of sentries at his base, and placed an especially alert sentry at his door day and night. Little did he know that the sentry in front of his door was the very spy he feared!

Get Your Memory Sleep

Your memory will be fresh as a daisy—if you are! Many researchers think that long-term memories only form when we are asleep. If you don't get enough shut-eye, expect your memory to wilt long before lights out.

Mole in the Hole

In 1951, the British Secret Service developed a plan to spy on Russia. Both countries had headquarters in Vienna, Austria. The British decided to dig a tunnel that would run underneath the Russian site. The plan was code-named Operation Silver. From the tunnel, the British were able to tap into Russian phone lines, then decode the messages they intercepted. Operation Silver was so successful that the plan was repeated as Operation Gold in Berlin, Germany!

Spy in the Sky

If you think U2 is just the name of a rock band, think again. *U2* was the name for top-secret spy planes launched by the U.S. in 1956. The planes flew at extremely high altitudes—over 20,000 metres (70,000 feet)—to escape both radar and missiles. That's twice as high as today's commercial airlines. Despite their altitude, the photos taken by the *U2*s were so accurate that you could count the number of golf balls on a course that appeared in the pictures!

I.C.U. Headquarters

TO: Agent Y.O.U.

FROM: Department of Cryptology

Your formidable skills in fitness, disguise, and surveillance have led you to this embedded training manual. You have been selected to participate in the introductory training program for cryptologists. Descriptive briefs on each page of the manual present different types of codes and ciphers. You must learn them all. Good luck!

top secret

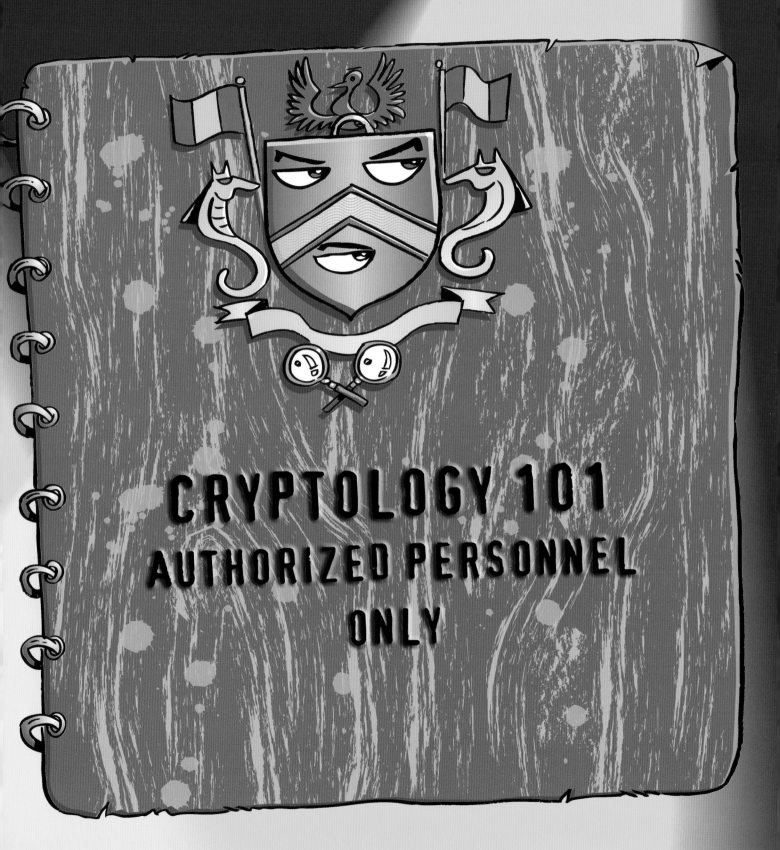

The Oldest Code in the Book

Code Type: Simple Substitution
Code Difficulty Level: 1

Brief: This simple substitution code is one of the most ancient codes we know of.

How It Works: Write out the alphabet in order from A to Z. Below it, write the alphabet in reverse order, from Z to A. Use the letters in the reversed alphabet to substitute for letters in your code. Example: A becomes Z, J becomes Q, and Y becomes B.

A B C D E F G H I J K L M N O P Q R S T U V W X Y Z
Z Y X W V U T S R Q P O N M L K J I H G F E D C B A

To Decode: Simply write the alphabets as above. Substitute the letters in the coded message for the corresponding letters in the regular alphabet.

Sample Coded Message:

TLLW HGZIG, OVGH PVVK TLRMT!

Answer on page 63.

Caesar Code

Code Type: Simple Substitution
Code Difficulty Level: 1

Brief: Code is named for Julius Caesar, a great military and political leader in ancient Rome, who used this code to communicate with his trusted associates.

How It Works: Encode your chosen message by shifting each letter three positions to the right in the alphabet. For example, MEET would be encoded to PHHW.

To Decode: Shift each letter of the code three positions to the left in the alphabet.

To Encode

X Y Z A B C D E F G H I J K L M N O P Q R S T U V W X Y Z A B C

To Decode

Sample Coded Message:

ZKHUH LV PB VDODG?

Answer on page 63.

Key Word Shift Code

Code Type: Substitution
Code Difficulty Level: 4

Brief: This is a substitution code in which letters are shifted, as in the Caesar Code. However, one must know a special word, called the key word, which begins the shift and indicates how many letters one must shift.

How It Works: Choose a key word that does not have any letters repeated in it, for example, TULIP. Write your alphabet along one row. Immediately under the A, begin writing your key word, with the T under A, the U under B, etc. The P will come under the E. Under F, begin writing the alphabet, **omitting the five letters that appear in tulip**. Your two alphabets will now look like this:

A B C D E F G H I J K L M N O P Q R S T U V W X Y Z

T U L I P A B C D E F G H J K M N O Q R S V W X Y Z

Substitute the coded alphabet, the one on the bottom, for the regular alphabet when writing your text. Example: A becomes T, F becomes A.

To Decode: Using the chosen key word, write out the alphabets as above. Match each letter in the code to the corresponding letter in the regular alphabet. Continue until you have all of the words completed.

Sample Coded Message:
D GKQR HY GKLFPO FPY.

Tip: Change your key word frequently to prevent discovery.

Answer on page 63.

Greek Box Code

Code Type: Number–Letter Substitution
Code Difficulty Level: 6

Brief: The ancient Greeks developed this code to make simple substitution codes more difficult.

How It Works: A 5-column, 5-row grid is created. The numbers 1 to 5 run alongside the left-hand column and above the top row. The boxes in the grid are filled with the letters of the alphabet, from left to right and top to bottom (like the flow of reading in a book). The letter Z, since it is uncommon, is omitted.

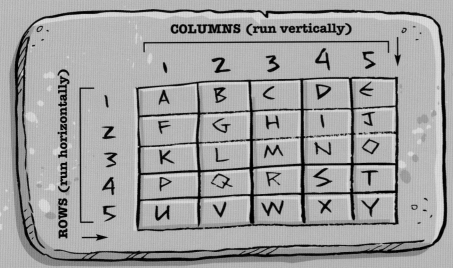

Each letter of the alphabet can now be described as a pair of number coordinates (always give the column number first). Column 1, row 1= A. Column 4, row 3= N. Write out each coded letter as a two-digit number and separate them with commas. For example, CAT would be written as 31, 11, 54.

To Decode: The receiver simply needs to create their own Greek Box to convert the number combinations back to letters.

Sample Coded Message: 42, 54, 44, 11, 23, 23, 22, 34, 51, 51, 13, 54, 53, 33, 51. Answer on page 63.

Rail Fence Code

Code Type: Simple Transposition Code
Code Difficulty Level: 4

Brief: Transposition codes change the order in which letters in words appear. The Rail Fence Code is named for the imaginary fence on which lines of the code sit.

How It Works: The coder decides how many "rails" (horizontal rows) she wants her fence to have. She then writes her message, placing each letter on the next row, or rail. When the last rail is reached, she continues the message at the top. The process continues until the end of the message is reached. The coder then prepares the message for delivery by presenting the letters of each row as a separate "word."

Example: If the message is, "We are having beans for dinner," and the coder wanted to use a three-rail fence, she would write out the message like this (add Xs to fill out remaining blank boxes at the end of the message):

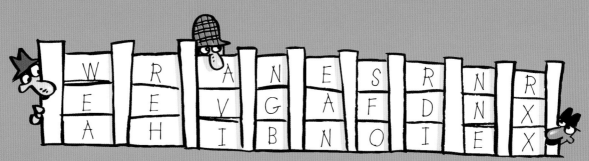

Then, the coder rewrites the message, each new "word" representing a row. Thus, the new coded message reads as a three-word message: WRANESRNR EEVGAFDNX AHIBNOIEX.

To Decode: Count the number of "words" in the coded message. This tells you how many rails to use. Write each word of the message on each rail of the fence. To read, read down the columns.

Sample Coded Message: TEFIO HSENU ENNGI ROCYN!
Answer on page 63.

Date Shift Code

Code Type: Polyalphabetic Substitution
Code Difficulty Level: 7

Brief: In this code, you use today's date, specified in numerals, to define how many positions in the alphabet you shift each individual letter in your message. Because there is more than one shift used in this code, it is much more difficult to break than simple substitution codes.

How It Works: Write out your message. Then write a numeral of the date underneath each letter of your message, repeating the date as many times as necessary. So, if the date were July 14, 2015 (7142015) the setup would look like this:

I'LL   SEE YOU AT SEVEN
7'14   201 571 42 01571

Based on the pairing of letters and numbers, each letter of your message shifts to the **right** according to the number indicated below it. In the example above, the letter I would shift 7 letter positions to become P; the second letter, L, would become M; and the third letter, another L, would be P! If you get to the end of the alphabet before you have finished counting, continue from A until you have reached the target number for the substitution. Send the coded message in the form of an everyday note, dated at the top.

To Decode: Write the date under the coded message, and shift each letter to the **left** that number of places. If you get to the beginning of the alphabet before you have finished counting, go all the way around to Z and keep moving backward.

Sample Coded Message: using the same date as above, July 14, 2015 (7142015): AIMU IT YVVKJ! Answer on page 63.

Yellow Brick Road Code

Code Type: Transposition Code
Code Difficulty Level: 8

Brief: Letters of the message are filled into a grid. They are then transposed according to a predetermined path, such as a spiral.

How It Works: The coder writes a short message in a grid, working from left to right and top to bottom. She then decides on a key path, for example, a clockwise spiral. The coder draws the path through the boxes. She then writes the letters from each of the boxes in order as they appear along the path. Happy trails! The text is now in code.

Example: The message is, "I have the spying equipment." The message is written in the grid, adding Xs to fill any leftover spots. The coder then adds the desired path. Here, a clockwise spiral:

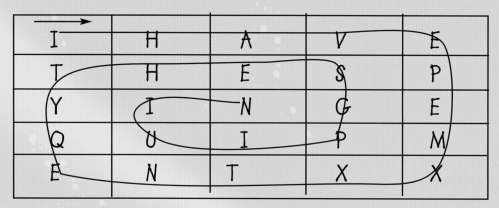

The message is then written out by indicating the dimensions of the grid followed by the letters as they appear along the path, like this: 5x5=IHAVEPEMXXTNEQYTHESGPIUIN. Include a small drawing of the path, indicating the direction of movement with an arrow, with the message.

To Decode: Draw a 5 x 5 grid. Then draw the key shape onto the grid, making sure to follow the direction of movement. Plot the letters of the message in order along the path. Read across each row from left to right, all the way down the grid.

Sample Coded Message:
5x5=XDVRRAUOYEYEXXXXIEEVACRKL!

I.C.U. Headquarters

&

the Department of Cryptology
in association with Fairleigh Ridiculous University
Recognize that

Agent Y.O.U.

has met all the requirements necessary for the completion of the
top-secret, classified, and really, really hard program in

Cryptanalysis

By the power given to the Department of Cryptology by someone in a really
high-up position, you are hereby allowed to call yourself by the official title of

Dr. of Decodery

Degree Granting Authority

I.C.U. Representative

Fact File

Ultra-Human Code Crackers

During World War II, the Germans used devices called Enigma machines to create codes. One of the most important challenges for the Allied forces in the fight against Nazi Germany was breaking the Enigmas' codes. Bletchley Park, a sprawling English mansion, was set up as a code-analysis facility. Most of the Bletchley Park code breakers had unusual talents; some were chess champions, others crossword experts, great mathematicians, or superb linguists. The intelligence that was gathered by cracking the German codes at Bletchley Park was called ULTRA, because it was given the highest-ranked level of secrecy.

Back to the Drawing Board

In 2005, Xiaoyun Wang, a Chinese cryptographer at Tsinghua University in Beijing, made international news when she cracked the toughest code in digital security—the code used to make Websites safe for credit card transactions, protect passwords, and authenticate digital signatures. The code, called SHA-1, was considered by the U.S. National Security Agency (NSA) to be next to impossible to break. Rumor has it she is now working on cracking that age-old puzzle: Which came first, the chicken or the egg.

A Wheely Great Prez

Thomas Jefferson, the third president of the United States, is widely credited with developing a coding device called the Jefferson Cipher Wheel. The device uses scrambled alphabets on several wheels to encode a message. The wheels are individually numbered and then placed on a spindle in any prearranged order. Because the wheels can be arranged in many ways, coded texts produced using this device are very tough to decrypt.

Purple was Her Favorite Color?

Genevieve Feinstein always wanted to become a math teacher. In 1939, however, she was offered a job as a U.S. government cryptanalyst to try to decode Japanese military communications. Japan used a code machine called PURPLE. Just prior to the United States' involvement in World War II, Feinstein made a breakthrough that changed the course of history. Her work enabled the U.S. to build a machine that could decipher the Japanese codes. It is believed that cracking PURPLE's codes contributed to the Allied forces' Pacific victory.

51

COMMUNICATION,
SPY-STYLE

You did it! You've got the top-top-secret plans of the enemy's space pod facility. All that remains now is for you to get them into your contact, Penelope Pluto's, hands.

Easier said than done. The enemy is everywhere, watching your every move. How will you get the plans to Pluto? In this confidential communiqué, you will be briefed on everything you need to master the art and science of communication, spy-style.

PLUNGER
LIZARD LIPS
BUGABOO!

DOUGHNUT

TOE JAM

Identifying Your Contact

As an agent in the field, Y.O.U. have never seen another member of your network. How will you recognize Agent Pluto when you meet?

Spies have developed many ingenious techniques for solving this identity dilemma. A secret password, known only by your allies, is one of the oldest tricks in the spook book.

Create Your Own Secret Password

Making a secret password for your own spy network is easy. Choose a word or phrase that is easy to remember. Don't write it down! You might consider selecting a word at random from the dictionary. Change your password frequently in case someone accidentally overhears you when you use it.

BASEBALL

PINK FLAMINGO

CORDUROY

Let's Shake on It

A secret handshake is another great way to make sure your contact is who they are supposed to be. The best kind is one that both hand-shakers can feel, but which others can't see. It should also be subtle, so if it turns out you have the wrong person, they don't catch on to what you are doing.

Try this one, or modify it to make up your own.

▷ When you shake hands, tickle the inside of the other person's palm with your pinky finger.

▷ His response should be to quickly squeeze your thumb.

If the other person does not respond correctly, return your finger to its normal position and continue with a regular handshake.

The Mix 'n' Match Greeting

To guarantee the right people connect, spies are sometimes given one half of an object, such as a ripped coupon or a playing card. If the two halves match up, chances are good the meeting is safe.

The No-Meet Meet

Passwords and handshakes work well when you and your colleagues are all together. But how do you get your network together in the first place? You need a prearranged signal, one that does not rely on any of you being in the same place at the same time for sending and receiving it.

Get together with your spy network and agree ahead of time on what your meeting place will be (say, a treehouse in your backyard). Next, choose a method for contacting each other and what each signal will mean. Try these methods:

▷ Make a chalk mark on the sidewalk outside of your meeting place. A green chalk mark means, "Meet at the treehouse after school." A red chalk mark might mean, "The treehouse is closed today."

▷ Leave a newspaper or comic book in the school library, opened to page 10 to tell your colleagues to get together at recess.

▷ A phony email message with a signal embedded in it can be both effective and funny. Example: Address your email to "My dear Prairie Dogs" to let your spy network know you want to meet to welcome a new member.

Delivering the Message

You've arranged the meet. Now you have to deliver the goods. The brush pass and the dead drop are two methods for trading secrets with your contact. Two methods with endless possibilities....

The Brush Pass

The brush pass is a lot like passing the baton in a relay race. It relies on good timing, excellent acting skills, solid planning, and a little bit of luck. Here are three agent-approved methods to try:

The Classic Klutz
Saunter past your contact on the street. Drop something, such as your notebook. Of course it has the message tucked inside the front cover. Your contact picks up the book and hands it back to you, while at the same time she removes the message.

The Fido
Fold your message so it fits under your dog's collar. Walk the dog. Meet your contact who asks if he can pet the dog. You say yes, and when he does, he removes the message from the collar. Then you both continue in opposite directions.

The Future Olympian
Go to the park to "practice your soccer skills." Tape your message to the ball. "Inadvertently" kick the ball over to where your contact is sitting. Have her pick up the ball and remove the message before she tosses it back to you.

Dead Drop
A dead drop is a prearranged location where you leave the secret goodies for your contact to retrieve later. Almost any place can be used for a dead drop. For a dead drop to work, choose your location carefully. It should not be likely to be disturbed by other people or animals. If it is outside, it must be protected from the elements.

Hiding Messages

Savvy field agents need to know how to conceal their stash.

The Double Decker

With this double-crosser of a card trick, you can deliver maps and secret documents (e.g. a letter or a map) right under the Queen of Hearts' nose!

You'll Need

secret document
pencil
ruler
scissors
glue stick
two identical decks of standard playing cards (make sure no one will ever want to use them again—they will get ruined)

1 Cut your secret document into 6 cm x 8 cm ($2\frac{1}{2}$ in. x $3\frac{1}{4}$ in.) rectangular pieces. Each piece should be slightly smaller than a playing card.

2 Collect a matching pair of cards from the two decks for each piece of your document. Set the remaining cards of one deck aside. Carefully glue one piece of the document onto the face of a card from each pair. Allow to dry 10 minutes.

3 Apply a thin layer of glue to the exposed edges of the card. (You want the glue to hold, but it should still be easy enough for your contact to separate the cards.) Carefully lay the matching card face side up over the document to make a sandwich.

4 Let the glue dry completely (about 20 minutes). Then insert the secret cards back into the deck you set aside in step 2.

5 Deliver the deck to your contact.

Your contact can then go through the deck and find the thicker cards, separate the two halves of the sandwich, and reassemble the message!

Newspaper Pin-Prick Message

What's more common than a daily newspaper? No one will suspect a thing if you pass on a message using a day-old or a free community newspaper.

You'll Need
paper & pencil
day-old newspaper or a free community newspaper
safety pin

1 Write out a draft of your message on the piece of paper.

2 Find a day-old newspaper. Look for an example of each word in your message—this will be easier for you and your contact if the message is brief and simple.

3 Using the safety pin, prick a tiny hole underneath each of the words. Try to keep the words in the same order as the words in your message.

4 Give the newspaper to your contact (consider a brush pass or dead drop). All she has to do is hold the paper up to a light source (i.e. sunshine) to find the pinholes and read your message.

I'LL BRING THE VIDEO, YOU BRING THE SNACKS

Invisible Ink

The time-honored method of hiding messages is to write them in invisible ink. Whip up a batch of this ghostly potion quickly and easily at home.

You'll Need
measuring cup
125 mL ($\frac{1}{2}$ cup) baking soda
125 mL ($\frac{1}{2}$ cup) water
plastic spoon
small plastic bowl
2 small paintbrushes or 2 cotton swabs
plain white paper
small plastic cup
125 mL ($\frac{1}{2}$ cup) purple grape juice from concentrate

1 Mix the baking soda and water together in the bowl. Stir with the spoon.

2 Dip the paintbrush or cotton swab into the baking soda/water mixture. Write your message on the paper, leaving lots of space between each letter so they don't run together. Dip the brush or swab after each letter to ensure a clear message.

3 Allow the message to dry. It takes about 15 minutes, but you'll know.

4 Carefully pour the grape juice into the cup. To reveal the message, lightly paint over the paper with grape juice using a clean brush or swab. The message will magically appear!

Remember...
grape juice stains, and the best spies leave no trace, so work neatly.

59

Fact File

The Navajo Code Talkers

The Navajo language of the southwestern Native American nation is so complex that no one but a native Navajo speaker can really get it right. During World War II, the Navajo language acted like a communication code. The Allied forces recruited Navajo speakers to work as radio operators. Their back and forth messages—many of them containing critical information about troop movements—were plainly heard by the enemy code breakers. It didn't matter. The Germans couldn't even *begin* to decipher what was being said. The Navajo "code" was never broken.

Message Will Self-Destruct in 10...9...8...

A service available to cellphone subscribers allows text messagers to send messages that, like time bombs, blow themselves up! The service is for people who want to send sensitive information, but are afraid that it might fall into the wrong hands. Intelligence sent using "stealthtext" erases itself after 40 seconds, leaving no trace for snoops.

Please Enter Your Password

Passwords are useful outside of your secret agent work too. Passwords are vital when you work on-line. You need passwords to protect your email accounts, your Internet transactions, even your very identity.

When choosing a password for the Internet, don't use something easy to guess like your nickname, the name of your pet, or your birthday. Pick a word or number at random, but one that Y.O.U. can remember easily. Don't share it with anyone (except your parents, of course)!

Winged Warriors

During World War I and II, one of the most reliable ways to deliver messages was by using homing pigeons. These avian soldiers were specially outfitted with unbreakable, lightweight canisters for the notes. Messages had to be very short (tissue-thin paper was used for maps), and codes were often written in teensy type. Some birds even received medals for valor. Amazingly, nearly all of the pigeons sent through enemy fire completed their missions.

I.C.U. Headquarters

Dear Agent Y.O.U.

You have now successfully completed all of the required training for promotion. Congratulations on a job well done!

Here is your next assignment: It is a critical one, on which the security of the entire world depends. Your mission, if you accept it, will make you a sleeper agent. You will go about your day-to-day business. To all others, you will appear as an ordinary kid. But when the time comes for you to save the world, you will be recalled to action. So stay fit, maintain your mental sharpness in school, and keep your eyes open. You never know when we will need to call upon your talents. Stay ready!

We know you can handle this mission. Good luck!

Mission Answers

p. 7: Talk the Talk

1. Birdwatcher, e)
2. Babysitter, j)
3. Cobbler, h)
4. Disinformation, c)
5. Rolled up, a)
6. Musician, f)
7. Shoe, d)
8. Sleeper, b)
9. The take, i)
10. Uncle, g)
11. Mole, k)

p. 8–9: Spy World

a) Cryptologist
b) Forensic expert
c) Case officer
d) Communications officer
e) Mole
f) Electronics technician
g) Counter intelligence officer
h) Spymaster
i) Sleeper agent
j) Technical officer
k) Surveillance officer
l) Surreptitious entry specialist
m) Linguist
Bonus: The jib is beside the red car.

p. 13: The Paris Train Challenge
Mission Report Card

If you stopped jumping or jogging before the 3 minutes were up—Say, "cheese." N.M.E. H.Q. now has your picture on file, your courier requests a team transfer, and you did not save the world. Improve your aerobic capacity to ensure future missions go smoothly! Practice jumping rope—a little bit at a time every day—until you can complete this mission.

If you completed the 3-minute mission, but are out of breath, sweating like mad, red in the face, and your heart is pounding like a rock band—Luckily your courier was able to hold the train for a moment, and the world has survived by a hair. For greater safety in future missions, improve your aerobic capacity. Gradually increase your jumping/jogging time from 3 to 5 minutes daily.

If you completed the 3-minute mission with only a little huffing and puffing—Good work, Agent Y.O.U. Your photograph is nothing but a blur, and you catch your breath as you take a seat and take in your surroundings on the train. Maintain and improve your aerobic fitness by jumping/jogging at least 10 minutes daily and doing other forms of physical exercise every day.

p. 15: Poison Dart Challenge
Mission Report Card

If you scored 160+—You're kabobbed! Luckily, you were wearing your poultry-proof vest or you would have been—gulp—skewered.

If you scored 100–160—Chicken fricassee! The poison dart missed you by a beak.

If you scored 40–100—That chicken got fried! Not only did you dodge the dart, but in the same instant you caught it in one hand, added a stamp, and diverted the poisoned poultry to N.M.E. headquarters.

p. 17: Losing the Tail
Mission Report Card

If you scored 160 seconds or more—You're not quite a gazelle. So agility isn't your strongest suit. Don't worry—when the agents caught you, the microdisc was long gone—passed off to another agent when you stopped to bite into a foot-long hotdog.

If you scored 80–100 seconds—You're an artful dodger. Your impressive fakes and dodges helped you lose your enemies, but you bumped into six soccer hooligans along the way. Better keep moving!

If you scored 60 seconds or less—Leapin' lizards! You lost your tail before you even reached the exits. The microdisc is safe.

p. 19: The Jittery Jewel Thief Affair
Mission Report Card

If you ring the buzzer before the halfway mark—You really should stop drinking those caffeine drinks! Those shaky hands nearly got the world exploded! Luckily, the radon wires malfunctioned and instead of causing a nuclear meltdown, the air conditioning just went off.

If you get halfway along the wire before the buzzer rang—Just as you lifted the diamond off of the stand, Dr. Repento's wiener dog barked and startled you, forcing you to drop the diamond. Luckily, your cuff missed the radon wires, the diamond bounced into your pocket, and your mission was completed.

If you get the whole way along the wire without buzzing—The diamond is safe! Dr. Repento was thrown into his guppy tank, the evil henchmen were disarmed, and you didn't even mess up your hair.

Too Easy? Increase the difficulty of this mission by adding more bumps and curves to the hanger or by decreasing the size of the foil loop.

p. 32: The Pattern Game

If you let it go—Tut, tut! Your observation antennas need a little fine-tuning. Drinking champagne and dancing by oneself don't seem like typical behavior for anyone. Next time, make the report and let your superiors decide what's going down.

If you report Agent RV—Well done! RV has exhibited some unusual behavior, such as forgetting the bread, neglecting to walk the dog, meeting others for lunch, and drinking champagne. This may indicate that she has made a deal to sell valuable state secrets. Or, that she won the lottery.

p. 33: Liar, Liar Pants on Fire

Johnnie's downcast eyes and rigid body position give him away—he's the liar.

p. 34: Mind Your Memories

a) True
b) One pair of eyes
c) Two people with moustaches
d) True
e) The bride
f) False
g) Mountains

If you got fewer than four answers correct, keep practicing Mission 4-1 (page 31) to boost your powers of observation.

p. 42–43:

The Oldest Code in the Book—Good start, let's keep going!
Caesar Code — Where is my salad?

p. 44–45:

Key Word Shift Code—I lost my locker key.
Greek Box Code—It's all Greek to me.

p. 46–47:

Rail Fence Code—There's no fencing you in!
Date Shift Code—This is tough!

p. 48–49:

Yellow Brick Road Code!—You are a very clever kid!

Index